AMAZING AMPHIBIANS

TREE FROGS

JAMES E. GERHOLDT

Published by Abdo & Daughters, 4940 Viking Drive, Suite 622, Edina, Minnesota 55435.

Library bound edition distributed by Rockbottom Books, Pentagon Tower, P.O. Box 36036, Minneapolis, Minnesota 55435.

Printed in the United States.

Cover Photo credit: Peter Arnold
Interior Photo credits: Animals Animals, pages 5, 6, 9, 11, 14-19, 21
James Gerholdt, pages 6, 7, 8, 10, 13, 14, 20
Page 14 courtesy of Minnesota Zoo

Edited by Julie Berg

LIBRARY OF CONGRESS CATALOGING-IN-PUBLICATION DATA

Gerholdt, James E., 1943—
    Tree frogs / James E. Gerholdt.
        p.   cm. -- (Amazing amphibians)
    ISBN 1-56239-311-1
    1. Hy 1 idae--Juvenile literature.   [1. Tree frogs. 2. Frogs]
    I. Title. II. Title: Tree frogs. III. Series: Gerholdt, James E.,
    1943- Amazing amphibians.
    QL688.E2G47   1994
    597.8'7--dc20
                                        94-18099
                                        CIP
                                        AC

CONTENTS

TREE FROGS

Tree frogs are amphibians. Amphibians are ectothermic. This means they get their body temperature from the environment. Tree frogs like it cool. If they get too hot, they will die. And if they are too cool, their bodies won't work. Tree frogs also need moisture or they will dry up and die. There are over 800 species found in the world. They are found almost everywhere. Tree frogs usually have smooth skin and long legs with suction cups on their toes.

This South American tree frog is climbing a plant.

This Shovel-nosed tree frog is found in Mexico.

SIZES

Some tree frogs grow to be very large. The White's tree frog from Australia can have a body 4 inches long. The White-lipped tree frog from Indonesia is almost as large. But most species are much smaller. The tiny Squirrel tree frog from the southeastern United States can be full-grown at less than 1 inch. But most of the tree frogs are from 1 to 2 inches in length.

The White's tree frog from Australia grows to be very large.

*The tiny Squirrel tree frog from the
United States is one of the smallest of all tree frogs.*

SHAPES

Tree frogs come in many different shapes. Some, like the White's and Cuban tree frog, are round and fat. Other species, such as the Green tree frog from the United States, are much more slender. But what makes a tree frog different from other frogs is their toes. They have suction cups! These let them climb up almost any surface they want to. On a rainy summer night you might even see one on the outside of your window!

The Green tree frog from the United States is a slender species.

This Orange-eyed tree frog from Costa Rica is using the suction cups on its toes to climb.

COLORS

Many tree frogs have colors that help them blend in with their surroundings. This is called camouflage. And some can change from gray to green and back to gray again. On a tree trunk, gray blends in, and on a leaf, green blends in. Some species are always green, and when sleeping, they look like a leaf. One of the most colorful tree frogs is the Red-eyed tree frog from Central America.

***This Western chorus frog from Minnesota
blends in with the background.***

The Red-eyed tree frog from Central America is brightly colored.

HABITAT

Tree frogs need moisture to live. But many are found far from water. The Green tree frog lives on plants near water and sleeps on the underside of the leaves. Other species spend most of their lives near the tops of trees. The Gray tree frog is often found on the trunks of trees, and also on the sides of houses. The Cuban tree frog lives on plants, and as a result, is sometimes sent far from home attached to them. That's why this species is often found in nurseries and greenhouses.

This Gray tree frog from Minnesota is at home on tree trunks.

This Cuban tree frog from Florida spends much of its time sitting on plants.

SENSES

Tree frogs and humans have the same 5 senses. Tree frogs' eyesight is very good. They can see their enemies before it is too late to get away. The eyes have special glands to keep them moist and have movable eyelids to protect them. Right in front of the nose is a blind spot, so they must turn their heads to see directly ahead. Their hearing is also good, which helps them to find their mates.

You can see the large eardrum on this White-lipped tree frog from Indonesia.

This Lemur frog from Costa Rica has very large eyes.

DEFENSE

The most important defense of most tree frogs is their camouflage. But if they are seen by their enemies, they can jump onto another plant or tree to escape. Some of the tree frogs can actually glide through the air, just like a flying squirrel. Species that glide are found in South America and Asia. Heavy webbing between their toes helps them to glide. Other species, like the Cuban tree frog, have skin secretions that will irritate the mouth of an enemy.

This Green tree frog can jump to escape its enemies.

The foot of this Wallace's flying frog is heavily webbed.

FOOD

Tree frogs will eat almost anything that moves and will fit into their mouths. They all eat other animals: insects, spiders, worms, or small mammals. The White's tree frog from Australia likes eating mice, while the smaller species enjoy crickets. If the tree frogs see a movement, they will jump down, grab, and swallow. They might even eat a smaller tree frog! But while the adults eat other animals, the tadpoles eat algae and other plants found in the water.

This Red-eyed tree frog is jumping after a cricket.

This Gray tree frog from the United States is enjoying a tasty cricket.

BABIES

Most tree frogs lay their eggs in the water. Depending on the species, there may be from 10 to 3,000 eggs. These hatch into tadpoles (polliwogs). After a few weeks to 2 months, these metamorph (change) into tiny frogs and then leave the water. Other species lay their eggs on leaves above the water. When they hatch, the tadpoles wiggle free and drop into the water. Other species build a foam nest made from the female's fluid, and lay their eggs in this nest. When the tadpoles hatch, they wiggle free and fall into the water.

This Spring peeper from Minnesota is calling to attract a female.

These Red-eyed tree frog eggs were laid on a leaf in Panama.

Gray tree frog tadpole in its first stage of life.

GLOSSARY

Amphibians (am-FIB-i-ans) - scaleless animals with backbones that need moisture to live.

Algae (AL-gee) - a plant without a stem that grows in the water.

Camouflage (CAM-o-flaj) - the ability to blend in with the surroundings.

Ectothermic (ek-to-THERM-ik) - regulating body temperature from an outside source.

Environment (en-VI-ron-ment) - surroundings an animal lives in.

Habitat (HAB-e-tat) - an area an animal lives in.

Metamorph (MET-a-morf) - change from a larval to an adult form.

Polliwog (POLL-ee-wog) - a larval frog or toad.

Suction cups - things that stick to a smooth surface.

Tadpole (TAD-pole) - a larval frog or toad.

Index

A

algae 18
Asia 16
Australia 6, 18

B

babies 20

C

camouflage 10, 16
Central America 10
Cuban tree frog 8, 12, 13, 16

D

defense 16

E

eggs 20
eyesight 14

F

flying squirrel 16

G

Gray tree frog 12, 19, 21
Green tree frog 8, 12, 16

H

hearing 14

I

Indonesia 6

L

Lemur frog 15

O

Orange-eyed tree frog 9

P

polliwogs 20

R

Red-eyed tree frog 10, 11, 18, 21

S

Shovel-nosed tree frog 5
South American tree frog 4, 16
Spring peeper 20
Squirrel tree frog 6, 7
suction cups 4, 8

T

tadpoles 18, 20

U

United States 6, 8

W

Wallace's frog 17
White-lipped tree frog 6, 14
White's tree frog 6, 8, 18
Western chorus frog 10

About the Author

Jim Gerholdt has been studying reptiles and amphibians for more than 40 years. He has presented lectures and displays throughout the state of Minnesota for 9 years. He is a founding member of the Minnesota Herpetological Society and is active in conservation issues involving reptiles and amphibians in India and Aruba, as well as Minnesota.

Photo by Tim Judy